Thunderbirds Brains Ruled Notebook first published in Great Britain 2014
by Egmont UK Limited, The Yellow Building, 1 Nicholas Road, London W11 4AN
Thunderbirds ™ and © ITC Entertainment Group Limited 1964, 1999 and 2014.
Licensed by ITV Ventures Limited. All rights reserved.

ISBN 978 1 4052 7547 7
58533/1
Printed in China